HAL•LEONARD
INSTRUMENTAL
PLAY-ALONG

AUDIO
ACCESS
INCLUDED

PLAYBACK+
Speed • Pitch • Balance • Loop

TRUMPET

MOTOWN CLASSICS

To access audio visit:
www.halleonard.com/mylibrary

Enter Code
2231-4328-5333-2413

ISBN: 978-1-4584-0560-9

Visit Hal Leonard Online at
www.halleonard.com

Contact us:
Hal Leonard
7777 West Bluemound Road
Milwaukee, WI 53213
Email: info@halleonard.com

In Europe, contact:
Hal Leonard Europe Limited
42 Wigmore Street
Marylebone, London, W1U 2RN
Email: info@halleonardeurope.com

In Australia, contact:
Hal Leonard Australia Pty. Ltd.
4 Lentara Court
Cheltenham, Victoria, 3192 Australia
Email: info@halleonard.com.au

CONTENTS

ABC

TRUMPET

Words and Music by ALPHONSO MIZELL,
FREDERICK PERREN, DEKE RICHARDS
and BERRY GORDY

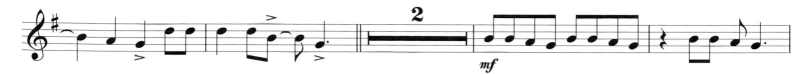

AIN'T NO MOUNTAIN HIGH ENOUGH

TRUMPET

Words and Music by NICKOLAS ASHFORD
and VALERIE SIMPSON

BABY LOVE

TRUMPET

Words and Music by BRIAN HOLLAND,
EDWARD HOLLAND and LAMONT DOZIER

ENDLESS LOVE

TRUMPET

Words and Music by
LIONEL RICHIE

HOW SWEET IT IS
(To Be Loved by You)

TRUMPET

Words and Music by EDWARD HOLLAND,
LAMONT DOZIER and BRIAN HOLLAND

I CAN'T HELP MYSELF
(Sugar Pie, Honey Bunch)

TRUMPET

Words and Music by BRIAN HOLLAND,
LAMONT DOZIER and EDWARD HOLLAND

I JUST CALLED TO SAY I LOVE YOU

TRUMPET

Words and Music by
STEVIE WONDER

I'LL BE THERE

TRUMPET

Words and Music by BERRY GORDY,
HAL DAVIS, WILLIE HUTCH
and BOB WEST

MY CHERIE AMOUR

TRUMPET

Words and Music by STEVIE WONDER,
SYLVIA MOY and HENRY COSBY

THREE TIMES A LADY

Trumpet

Words and Music by
LIONEL RICHIE

MY GIRL

TRUMPET

Words and Music by WILLIAM "SMOKEY" ROBINSON
and RONALD WHITE

STOP! IN THE NAME OF LOVE

TRUMPET

Words and Music by LAMONT DOZIER,
BRIAN HOLLAND and EDWARD HOLLAND

THE TRACKS OF MY TEARS

TRUMPET

Words and Music by WILLIAM "SMOKEY" ROBINSON,
WARREN MOORE and MARVIN TARPLIN

WHAT'S GOING ON

TRUMPET

Words and Music by RENALDO BENSON,
ALFRED CLEVELAND and MARVIN GAYE

YOU'VE REALLY GOT A HOLD ON ME

TRUMPET

Words and Music by
WILLIAM "SMOKEY" ROBINSON